SAY

YES, AND!

2 LITTLE WORDS That Will Transform Your Career, Organization, and Life!

AVISH PARASHAR

Printed in the United States of America

First Printing, 2012

ISBN 978-0-9833710-2-1

For Amanda, for saying, "Yes, And" to me
and changing my life forever...

THANKS

Many people have helped me put this book together. Not only in the specific act of the writing, but also in the years preceding when many of the ideas and principles were being (slowly) formulated. I am sure I am leaving some deserving people off, and if so, please accept my deepest apologies.

Thank you to Amanda Urbanczyk, Mike Worth, Chris Holmes, Erin Hyland, Fred Gleeck, Kendall Lin, Jenn Phillips, and David Newman. I couldn't have done it without you!

WHAT'S WAITING FOR YOU INSIDE

"YES, AND"

THE TRAP

One day I was driving with some friends on what could affectionately be called a "road trip." Two hours into the drive, the conversation turned to my business. One of my friends made a suggestion for a new service I could offer.

"Yes," I responded, "but that doesn't really fit in with what I want to do."

A second friend chimed in with a marketing idea.

"Yes, but that's pretty expensive, and doesn't really work for my market."

The third friend suggested I chat with some other people in a similar field who were further along than me.

"Yes, but their business models are different than mine. Besides, I don't want to bother them; why would they want to talk to me?"

After my third rejection of their good intentioned advice, they moved on to a new topic, quickly forgetting this brief exchange.

For me, however, the conversation lingered in my head.

It took me some time to realize that I had fallen into a trap.

It's a common trap that most, if not all, of us fall into all the time.

It's the trap of saying, "yes, but…"

THE "YES, BUT" PROBLEM

People are not as happy, successful, friendly, or fulfilled as they want and deserve to be.

You don't have to go very far to see it. Stories of horrible customer service, leadership, teamwork, sales, etc. are everywhere. Look around and you'll see countless people who have left behind their passions or given up on their dreams. Nastiness and negativity are so pervasive that you don't bat an eye when you see it.

As you read this, you yourself may be dissatisfied with some area (or multiple areas) of your life.

This is not to say that everyone, everywhere is a miserable failure. Not at all.

But everyone – you, me, the people around us – will occasionally (sometimes frequently) do things that hold us back, make our lives more difficult than they need to be, and ultimately lead to us living below our potential.

Even if you are doing quite well, standing on top of the world, you may be looking forward with trepidation and uncertainty, wondering, "What's next?"

In a nutshell, these problems can be summed up in two words: "Yes, but…"

So many problems occur simply because people choose to say, "yes, but" to life, to each other, and even to themselves.

The key to avoiding these problems is surprisingly simple. Instead of saying, "yes, but," say, "Yes, And." Two little words that can have a huge impact.

The process for saying, "Yes, And" is straightforward:

Make "Yes, And" your default mindset
Say "Yes, And" whenever you can.
Only "yes, but" after you have tried to say, "Yes, And."
What does saying, "Yes, And" mean?

It means exactly what it sounds like. When you find yourself saying, "yes, but," stop yourself and say, "Yes, And" instead.

THAT'S IT? JUST CHANGE ONE WORD?

Yes, that's it. It's only changing one word, but that one word makes a huge difference.

"Yes, And" is a way of thinking, speaking, and interacting with others that keeps you open-minded, allows you to act upon opportunities, helps you innovate, and allows you to fulfill your potential.

All that from two words?

Yes. All that from two words. But as with so many things, those two words are easier said than done…

"YES, AND" VS. "YES, BUT"

Most of the world doesn't say "Yes, And." Instead, people like to say "yes, but," which is the opposite of "Yes, And." "Yes, And" is positive, moves things forward, opens minds, and explores possibilities. "Yes, but" is negative, stops all forward progress, shuts down the mind, and cuts off creativity.

This is not just a logical distinction. Saying, "Yes, And" actually *feels* very different than saying, "yes, but."

Try a simple exercise with a partner: Have a conversation together, but after the first sentence have every sentence start with the two words, "yes, but." Then repeat the conversation, starting with the same first sentence, but this time have every sentence start with the two words, "Yes, And."

I guarantee you will not only notice a difference in the quality of the conversation, but you will also notice a palpable difference in how you feel, on a visceral level. After saying and hearing, "Yes, And," you will feel positive, supported, and collaborative. After saying and hearing, "yes, but," you will feel negative, attacked, and argumentative.

Those feelings exist in every conversation you have. What kind of feeling do you want to create in your communications?

DEFINING THE "YES, BUT" PROBLEM

You may be wondering, "what's the problem with saying, 'yes, but'?"

On the surface, this may not seem like a major issue. It's only a one-word difference, and frankly, does it really matter if it's a little negative?

It does. Saying, "yes, but" may seem harmless on the surface, but habitual use of the phrase can cause many problems:

- You will stay stuck where you are, rather than innovating.
- You will be closed minded and miss opportunities to do, see, and be more.
- You will negatively impact your relationship with everyone around you.
- You will drive away customers and prospects.
- You will be paralyzed when things don't go according to plan.
- You will increase your stress levels.
- You will wake up one day and say, "what happened to all those things I meant to do?"

Those are just a few. As you go through this book, you'll see many more drawbacks to being a "yes, but" person.

"YES, BUT" IS "NO" WITH A POLITE FACE

Face it: when you say "yes, but," you are just trying to politely say, "no." Just because the word "yes," comes out of your mouth doesn't mean that you actually mean it. The "but" eliminates the positive effective of the "yes."

Leaders of all levels, from CEOs to front-line managers, use this technique all the time. Rather than getting in a long discussion, they simply say, "yes, but" and go about their business. Making decisions is a good leadership trait; reflexive negativity masked with a smile is not.

If you want to say "no," say, "no." If you want to do something awesome, say, "Yes, And."

HOW DO YOU LIKE THE WORLD TO RESPOND TO YOU?

If you are uncertain whether "Yes, And" is a superior way to approach the world than "yes, but," consider your own experiences:

- When you step up to a customer service counter to return an item for which you have lost the receipt, do you prefer the person on the other side to say, "yes, but without a receipt you can not return it," or "Yes, And let me see what I can do for you"?
- When you get excited about an idea you have for your company and share it with your manager, do you want him to say, "yes, but we don't have the budget," or "Yes, And this is an interesting idea. Tell more about it and let's see if we can make it work"?
- When you need help with a problem, do you like it when people say, "yes but that's not my job," or do you prefer, "Yes, And let me see if I can direct you to someone who can help you"?
- When you tell your spouse, partner, or significant other about what you need from them, do you prefer it if they respond with, "yes, but that's not who I am," or do you prefer, "Yes, And I will do my best because I love you and want to make you happy"?
- When you are chatting with a salesperson and you raise an objection, how do you feel when he says, "yes, but your

objection is invalid because I have a solution"? Wouldn't you prefer him to say, "Yes, that is a legitimate concern, And let me share some solutions I have for that"?

- When you are brainstorming with colleagues, do you find it more productive when people respond to your ideas with, "yes, but that idea will never work," or when they say, "Yes, And here's another way we can build off of that idea"?

Take a look at your own life and preferences and it gets pretty obvious: "Yes, And" is a much better approach than "yes, but."

SAYING "YES, AND" TO YOURSELF

"Yes, And" is obviously how you want others to treat you, and should be the way you approach other people. But did you know that "Yes, And" matters for a much more important, much more personal reason?

The most insidious use of "yes, but" is not when an annoying customer service person brushes you off, or when a boss shoots down an idea, or when a loved one rejects something you are excited about. No, the worst use of "yes, but" is when you say it to yourself.

We, all of us, "yes, but" ourselves more than anyone else ever could. This makes a certain amount of sense. We are with ourselves 24 hours a day, 7 days a week. It stands to reason that we would say "yes, but" to ourselves more than anyone else:

- "I should go to the gym to workout. Yes but I am tired."
- "I should go talk to that interesting attractive person over there. Yes but they probably won't be interested in me."
- "I should put in an application for this promotion. Yes, but they would never hire me."
- "I should take evening classes to get my degree. Yes but I can't make the time for that."
- "I should [insert goal, dream, or aspiration]. Yes but [insert excuse]."

PLEASE LEARN FROM MY STUPIDITY!

The idea of saying, "Yes, And" instead of "yes, but," is very near and dear to my heart, because as I look back on my life I can say, without exaggeration, that everything I have right now came from saying, "Yes, And." And I almost missed out by being attached to saying "yes, but"…

My entire life now revolves around improv comedy. I have performed it for over twenty years. I ran my own group for seven years. I have a speaking and training business that uses improv comedy ideas to enable organizations to be more creative and communicate more effectively.

Would it surprise you to know that I got dragged into improv comedy kicking and screaming?

It's true. I "yes, butted" the heck out of improv comedy before I finally tried it. (What can I say? I can be a little dense).

Growing up, I had acted in all of my high school's theater productions. When I went off to college I decided not to get involved in theater because I knew what a time drain it was, and I wanted to "focus on my studies." (my parents would be so proud. They probably are now saying, "What the heck happened??") So, at college, I did not audition for or get involved in any performing arts groups.

After hanging out with my new college friends, one of them — his name is Matt, and he will never let me forget this story — suggested I try out for the university's improv troupe.

"Improv?" I said. "I don't do improv. I've always done scripted work. I don't think my humor would translate to improv."

Yes, that was me saying, "yes, but I don't think I'd be any good at it." Crazy.

What's truly ridiculous about my "yes, but" is that **I had never even seen the improv group perform!** I didn't really know what improv comedy was, but I knew it wasn't right for me. Like I said, I can be dense.

Matt, however, was an annoyingly persistent guy (thank goodness for that). He kept suggesting it to me, and every time he did, I would brush him off with a "no," or a resounding, "yes, but."

Finally, in a stroke of either sheer absurdity or sheer brilliance, he maneuvered me into going to see a show. It was almost like a romantic comedy; his friend was coming into town for a weekend, but Matt was busy Saturday night. Matt asked if I could hang with his friend so he wouldn't be bored. Being a good guy, I said, "sure," after which Matt slyly mentioned that the improv group happened to be having a show that night and we should go see it. Sneaky bastard…

We went to see the improv show, and within just a few minutes, I was hooked! I loved it, and really wanted to give it a try. When they held auditions a month later I tried out, got in, and improv has been a part of my life ever since.

To say that my life would be different if I had not finally said, "Yes, And" to auditioning for that improv group would be a gross understatement. I cannot imagine what my life would be like. In truth, I don't even want to imagine what my life would be like.

All because I finally stopped saying "yes, but" and said, "Yes, And."

EVERYTHING YOU HAVE IS A RESULT OF SAYING "YES, AND"

I am not trying to brag when I say that everything I have came from saying, "Yes, And." If you think about it, everything you have is a result of saying, "Yes, And" too.

Try this exercise: Take a piece of paper and draw a line vertically down the middle of it. On the left side, write down everything you have accomplished, everything you are good at, and everything you are proud of. On the right side, right down everything you wish you had done, everything you would like to be better at, and everything you consider a "failure."

Got your lists done? Good.

If you look at the left side of the page, you'll see that everything there came about because you said, "Yes, And." The right side of the page, the side of limitations, came about (or didn't come about) because you said, "yes, but."

You've already learned this lesson. Now it's time to apply it.

YOUR LIFE IS NOTHING
BUT A SERIES OF MOMENTS

In my improv comedy story above, my life changed for the better because in one moment, I said, "Yes, And" instead of "yes, but." In that story, I kept missing moments and stayed trapped in my "yes, but" world. Fortunately, I had annoyingly persistent people who kept throwing new moments at me until I finally said, "Yes, And."

I was immensely lucky. So often you don't get multiple chances. A moment hits and you have a choice of whether to say, "Yes, And" or "yes, but." If you say, "yes, but," that moment may very well be gone forever.

If I had not finally said "Yes, And" to attending that improv show, and later to auditioning for the group, my life would be drastically different. Everything that has happened in my life follows logically from that moment. I shudder to think what life would be like now if I had let it pass.

Our lives are long events that stretch over years and decades. However, when you think about it, our lives are nothing but a series of moments. Right now is a moment. And in fact, life is nothing but this moment right now. You cannot change the past or control the future; you can only act in this moment.

Since our lives are a series of moments, the quality of our lives is ultimately the result of how we act in each of those moments. Say, "yes, but" and your life will be a series of self-limiting beliefs and defeats. Say, "Yes, And" and you create a life of progress, opportunity, and success.

OPPORTUNITY IS LIKE
A DOOR TO DOOR SALESMAN

Opportunity knocks on your door, and if you don't open it then opportunity moves on and knocks on the next door. It doesn't keep pounding on your door for years until you wise up and answer.

I learned this lesson when some of my competitors chose to say, "yes, but," to an opportunity.

In the early days of my business, I got involved in the National Speakers Association. The group held meetings where experts from different fields would come in and share their experience and wisdom about the speaking business with us.

After one such meeting, I volunteered to give the presenter a ride back to the airport. Over the course of that 40 minute car ride, we realized we had some similar interests and decided we should try working together.

I was pretty new to the business, and he was well established, so this was a huge opportunity for me. I jumped at the chance.

A few days later I called him up on the phone and we chatted about how we could partner. Two months later I flew out to Las Vegas and we recorded a training DVD together. Since that time, we have continued to create products, run coaching programs, and deliver presentations together. That one moment turned into a terrific personal and business relationship.

What's interesting is that he told me I was not the first person he had made this offer to. In fact, he said he had made a similar offer to four other people in the past, but none of them followed up or did anything about it. Though I never spoke to any of those people about why they didn't follow through, I am pretty confident assuming that "yes, but" reared its ugly head.

For a special free gift, exclusively for book owners, visit: www.SayYesAnd.com/bookgift

"Yes, but I don't have time."

"Yes, but I'm not ready."

"Yes, but I'll do it later."

Frankly, I'm happy they did. Their "yes buts" opened the door for me to say, "Yes, And."

I wasn't necessarily any better than any of the others. I just happened to be the first one who said, "Yes, And."

If you want to make your competitors happy, be a "yes, but" person. They'll appreciate the chance to say, "Yes, And" and take your business away from you…

WHERE "YES, AND" COMES FROM

My background is in improv comedy. Improv comedy is a style of theater where the performers take the stage with nothing prepared in advance and work together to create comedy on the spot.

The idea of saying, "Yes, And" is fundamental to improv comedy. "Yes, but" blocks action. Interestingly, novice improvisers will commonly use "yes, but" to get a laugh.

You know what? It works. The audience will laugh. The problem is that "yes, but" stops the action in its tracks. By using "yes, but," the performer ruined an entire scene to get one laugh.

This is how "yes, but" manifests in our lives as well. Saying "yes, but" sometimes makes it very easy to get an immediate result in this moment, but it might do so at the cost of completely derailing your long term success.

Early on, competent instructors will teach their improv students to say, "Yes, And." Those two simple words let people improvise with any situation that happens on stage.

"Yes, but" is safe; "Yes, And" is effective. The same principle applies both on and off stage.

WHERE "YES, AND" REALLY COMES FROM

"Yes, And" did not originate with improv comedy. It's been around for a lot longer than that. In fact, saying, "Yes, And" is the natural order of things.

Consider young children. They don't have the capacity to think things over and talk themselves out of trying things. They just do what comes naturally to them. And for them, "natural" is saying "Yes, And."

Think about it: when a child learns to walk, she doesn't see others walking and say, "yes, but they are so much bigger than me!" She says, "Yes, And I would like to walk too!"

Every time she falls, she comes back with, "Yes, And I can do this" until she does.

It isn't until she gets older, and starts doubting herself, and starts letting her head get filled with messages of limitations, that she starts saying, "yes, but" to herself.

Maybe it's time to tap back into that childlike sensibility we all started with. Maybe it's time to say "Yes, And."

A WORD TO THE "REALISTS"

Right now you might be thinking, "well sure, "Yes, And" is a lovely idea in theory, but it's not practical. Sometimes you disagree with people. You can't just say, "yes, and" and agree to everything!"

You're right. Sometimes you do disagree. Sometimes the answer really is "no." "Yes, And," isn't about agreeing to everything. If the office slacker comes to you and says, "Oh hey, I have had this project for three weeks and I haven't done anything on it yet. Could you do it for me?" I am not suggesting that you say, "Yes, And let me pick up your dry cleaning too!" Not at all.

"Yes, And" is not a literal technique. You don't run around

suppressing your own thoughts and feelings and saying "yes," to everything, whether you agree or not.

"Yes, And" is a mindset. It is a way of approaching the world, other people, and even that little voice in your own head. Saying, "Yes, And" isn't about agreeing with everything; it's about making sure you don't disagree with everything out of hand. It's about staying open minded, exploring possibilities, and being willing to consider options you had not considered before.

So to the realists, you are right. If your wife or girlfriend comes to you and says, "Does this outfit make me look fat?" and you respond with, "yes, and old," you're on your own…

WHY YOU MAY SAY "YES, BUT"

If "yes, but" is so bad and limiting, why do so many people still use it? There are a few reasons:

Fear — Fear is the big one. People are afraid of change. They are afraid of the unknown. They are afraid of stretching and trying something new because they might fail. "Yes, but" keeps you nice and safe, and helps you avoid fear.

Short Term Thinking — "Yes, but" is almost always rooted in short term thinking. You say "yes, but" to opportunities because right now, you are too busy, too poor, too inexperienced, etc. to take advantage of them. "Yes, but" is also much more efficient in the short term. You can avoid conversations with people, and you can shut out everything you consider a distraction. Sadly, "yes, but" rarely accomplishes anything in the long term other than making certain that you make no progress in anything that is important to you.

Habit — If you have always said, "yes, but," it is possible that you have simply developed the habit of saying it. "Yes, but" reflexively comes out of your mouth when you are faced with a new challenge or opportunity. The first step in changing that habit is to be aware of it.

Lack of Knowledge — Some people never learn the value of saying "Yes, And" instead of "yes, but." To them, "yes, but" is the superior way to go because they have never analyzed and thought about other options. After reading this book, you can no longer use this as an excuse.

Lack of Clarity — If you lack clarity about your own desires and goals, you may "yes, but" things but not know why. This happens when you don't know what you want, but you do know what you don't want. Without clarity, you are unable to see the moments to say, "Yes, And" to. All you can do is continually shoot down every offer that comes your way. The way to get past this limitation is to sit down and figure out what it is you want. Then you can "Yes, And" to get it.

Need for Control — The most difficult aspect of saying, "Yes, And" for many is that in order to say it, you have to relinquish a little control. With "yes, but" everything can be exactly the way you want it. With, "Yes, And" you get other people's input, and they may change your idea, or take over parts of the project, or do things in a slightly different way. Don't assume this is a bad thing! Collaboration can be very powerful. Plus, the improved relationships you'll have will be well worth the little control you'll relinquish.

Belief in a Binary World — We are raised from a very young age to believe that things are either right or wrong. This is the way our educational system is set up; you either pass or fail. The answer is either right or wrong.

Ambiguity and interpretation are not often valued. As a result, people often end up as adults maintaining this either/or mentality. If I don't like some of your idea, I might say, "yes, but" to the whole thing. "Yes, And" requires a new form of thinking; you have to accept the fact that there might be more options than just "yes" or "no."

These are some reasons why people may say, "yes, but," but remember, they are reasons, not excuses! Just because you have a reason to say, "yes, but," doesn't mean you should!

For a special free gift, exclusively for book owners, visit: www.SayYesAnd.com/bookgift

"YES, AND"
COMMUNICATION

GOOD COMMUNICATION
IS AT THE HEART OF SUCCESS

If you are engaged in any activity that involves other people, in any way, then how well you communicate with those people directly impacts how successful you are in that activity.

If you and the people around you communicate well, things get accomplished, problems get resolved, and everyone stays happy. When communication is poor, progress stalls, problems spiral out of control, and everyone becomes miserable.

What's interesting is that the same idea applies even in endeavors that you engage in 100% on your own. Because, even if no one else is around, you are still constantly communicating with yourself. Your own internal communication style will greatly affect your own performance.

It then follows that, regardless of the type of activity you are engaging in, personal or professional, solo or with a team, the level of your success depends on the quality of your communication.

"Yes, And' is the simple tool you can use to increase the quality of your communication and make it as effective as possible.

"YES, BUT" MASQUERADING AS "YES, AND"

Saying, "Yes, And," isn't about language. It is about mentality, attitude, and approach. Just because you say, "Yes, And" doesn't mean that you mean "Yes, And."

If you are chatting with people about where to go to dinner and one person suggests a Chinese restaurant, saying, "Yes, And I don't really like Chinese food, let's go for Mexican," he is not really saying "Yes, And." You are really wrapping your "yes, but" in "Yes, And" clothing.

DO YOU NEVER SAY, "BUT"?

Of course not. "But" is a part of the English language and a fine word to use. "Yes, And" is superior, but if you must say "but" here are three important things to keep in mind:

1. **Say "yes, but" later!** Take some time to try to say "Yes, And." Have a "Yes, And" conversation first. Train yourself to reflexively think, "Yes, And." Then, after you have made a good, "Yes, And" attempt, you can say "but."

2. **Put the positive after the "but"!** The word "but" tends to invalidate whatever comes before it. If you say, "You did a great job on this report, but it's not formatted correctly," you place greater emphasis on the report's formatting. What the listener hears is, "my report was incorrect." You could say the exact same thing but change the meaning by switching it around: "This report isn't formatted correctly, but you did a great job." This becomes much more positive. What comes after the "but" is far more important than what comes before it. Make that the positive part.

3. **Use "but" to come up with alternatives!** If someone asks for your help and you can't help them, follow your declination

with, "but here are some other options that might work for you." That's saying, "but" with a "Yes, And" mentality.

THE "YES, BUT," VIRUS

One of the greatest dangers of "yes, but," is that it spreads. When one person repeatedly and emphatically says, "yes, but," not only does it create an atmosphere of negativity, but it can also beat the optimism and hope out of people who might otherwise be energetic and productive.

Sound too melodramatic? Think again…

THE "YES, BUT" BEATDOWN

Consider the story of Tim. Tim is an energetic young man who excitedly starts a job with a new company. After working for a little while, Tim starts generating ideas that he feels could help the entire company. He takes an idea to his boss who immediately says, "yes, that's a nice idea, but we don't have the money."

Tim leaves, a little dejected but not discouraged. A few weeks later he goes to his boss with another idea, to which his boss replies, "yes, that's a nice idea, but the higher ups will never go for it."

Tim returns to work, unsure of how to proceed, but he decides in another month to give another idea a try. Again, his boss responds with, "yes, that's a nice idea, but we are very busy right now and need to focus on current projects."

This goes on month after month, year after year, until Tim finally gives up suggesting ideas and buys into the "yes, but" mentality. Soon Tim is promoted to manager. One day he hires an energetic young woman named Stacey. Stacey, after working for a few months, comes into Tim's office with an exciting new idea that will surely benefit the entire company. Tim immediately responds with, "Yes, that's a nice idea, but we don't have the money…"

And on and on it goes. Tim has become another victim of the "yes, but" beatdown.

MAKING THE SWITCH

Am I saying that by simply switching from, "yes, but" to, "Yes, And" people can instantly improve their success, happiness, and relationships? Yes, yes I am.

It may not be easy to make the switch. You don't just start saying "Yes, And" and agree to everything. But by starting with "Yes, And" instead of "yes, but" you avoid the "yes, but" beatdown. Rather than crushing someone's hope, you listen to their ideas. You give them a chance to talk. You explore what they are saying. When you do this, a few things may happen:

- You may discover that the idea you were going to "yes, but" out of hand actually has a lot of merit and is worth pursuing.
- You may dig deeper into the idea and uncover previously hidden problems and solutions.
- You may create a third option that no one thought of before.
- You may ultimately realize that there is no workable solution and that you still have to say, "no."

However, when you have to say "no" after having properly applied the "Yes, And" approach, you have done so in a way that explored the idea, looked for options, and built respect and a connection with the person who made the request. People can accept being told "no" or "yes, but" if those words are preceded by a good "Yes, And" conversation.

"YES, AND" LETS YOU DIG DEEPER

"Yes, And" is an exploratory mindset. If someone comes to you with an idea for a new project, and you know out of hand that the idea will never work, you can certainly say, "yes, but." If you do that, however, you may miss out on a deeper, more important issue.

Often when someone comes to you with a suggestion, idea, or problem, what they are talking about is not what the real issue is. They may have an underlying reason or root cause that they are not verbalizing.

- This may be because they are hesitant to talk about it. Proper use of "Yes, And" can draw it out.
- This may because they don't know how to articulate what that underlying cause really is and they are just doing the best they can. By asking a good series of "Yes, And" questions you can help them formulate their thoughts.
- This may be because they aren't even aware that there is a deeper issue. "Yes, And" lets the two of you work together to uncover that issue and bring it to light.

"YES, AND WHY...?"

A simple way to dig deeper is to add a "why" to the end of "Yes, And." Rather than saying, "yes, but," say, "Yes, And why do you think this project is a good idea?"

After they answer, follow up with another "Yes, And why," and, if needed, another. And so on and so on.

Quite often, you can uncover root causes and deeper issues simply by asking a series of "Yes, And why..." questions.

Once the underlying reason or cause is uncovered, it can be addressed. However, if you don't take the time to dig deeper, you could very well waste time solving problems that don't need solving...

"YES, AND HOW ELSE…?"

A good follow up to the "Yes, And why…" conversation is the "Yes, And how else…" conversation.

Once you have dug deeper and found underlying reasons and root causes, asking, "Yes, And how else can we do that?" is an effective way to redirect a person away from their initial suggestion onto more efficient and effective ways of reaching their goals.

Doing this lets you be a resource to them. Instead of agreeing to everything out of hand, you help clarify and redirect so everyone gets what they want.

There is a difference between goals and tactics. Goals are what you are trying to achieve. Tactics are the methods you use to achieve those goals. "Yes, And how else…" helps you show someone how to achieve their original goal with different tactics.

Not only do you not say, "no" to them, but you also may very well help them find a better, faster, or more efficient way to achieve their goal.

"YES, AND" LETS YOU FIND THE THIRD OPTION

We live in a binary world. Computers are based entirely on bits being set to either 1 or 0. For some reason, we, as people, tend to fall into binary thinking as well. This is unfortunate because we are not computers; there are so many options available to us if we are just willing to be open minded enough to find them.

If someone comes to you with a suggestion, your immediate thoughts may fall into binary thinking. It is either, "yes, we accept your idea" or "no, we don't."

"Yes, And," however, allows you to find the third option.

For example, if you want to take a vacation in the mountains, and your spouse suggests you go to the beach, please realize that it doesn't have to be a binary, either/or decision.

Instead of immediately firing back with, "yes, but I want to go to the mountains!" use, "Yes, And" to find a third option.

For example:

- **"Yes, And why do you want to go to the beach?"** Maybe there's a mountain resort where you can get the same benefit.
- **"Yes, And can we do both?"** It never hurts to ask, and it's a smart move to start from this line of thinking.
- **"Yes, And why don't you go to the beach while I go to the mountains?"** This won't usually work when it comes to spousal vacations, but in many situations it can provide the perfect solution.
- **"Yes, And how can we make sure that we both end up happy?"** This is really what you're after.

"Yes, but" sets up an argument where one person will not be happy. "Yes, And" keeps your focus where it should be: finding a third option that makes everyone as happy as possible.

THE "YES, AND" CONVERSATION IS NOT A WASTE OF TIME

I know what you are thinking: "How can you expect me to waste time on a long "Yes, And" conversation if at the end of it I am going to say, "yes, but" anyway?"

First off, the "Yes, And" conversation doesn't have to be long. Five minutes of open-minded, focused attention can be enough to explore an idea sufficiently to determine whether it is worth pursuing.

Second, if you go into a "Yes, And" conversation "knowing you are going to say, "yes, but" anyway," then you are not approaching the conversation with the right mindset.

Third, while you may feel you are wasting time by having a "Yes, And" conversation now, you will actually be saving a great deal of time in the long run. Think of the amount of time you will save by not having to deal with miscommunication, resentment, and frustration. "Yes, And" heads off all of those things long before they become a problem.

Spend a little time up front with a "Yes, And" conversation and you can avoid the huge long-term time drains of repeated "yes, but" conversations.

USING
"YES, AND"

"YES, AND" IS WHERE SUCCESS HAPPENS

Consider this: No one achieved much of anything by staying in a "yes, but" mindset. At some point every great (and small) accomplishment anyone has ever had began with someone saying "Yes, And."

People say "yes, but" out of fear. They think that by "yes, butting" the world they can at least hold on to the success they already have. Sadly, this is not true at all.

The world is constantly changing and moving. Even if you say, "yes, but" in a desperate attempt to avoid change, the world will change without you. Your "yes, but" will soon be irrelevant and the world will pass you by.

LUKE SKYWALKER SAVED THE UNIVERSE BY SAYING "YES, AND"

In Star Wars, Luke Skywalker starts out as a big "yes, butter." Obi Wan Kenobi tells Luke to join him and learn the ways of the Force. Luke responds in a typical, "yes, but" fashion, saying he can't go because his aunt and uncle won't let him. Or they need him. Or whatever excuse young adults on the planet of Tatooine use to keep themselves from taking action.

Later, Luke discovers that Stormtroopers have killed his aunt and uncle and burned down their house. Realizing that now there is nothing holding him back, Luke finally says, "Yes, And," joins Obi Wan, and learns the way of the Force.

The rest is intergalactic history. Luke becomes a master Jedi, the Rebels defeat the Empire, and the universe is saved. All because Luke finally said, "Yes, And."

Can you imagine what would have happened if Luke had said, "yes, but I'm just a farm boy"? Princess Leia would never have been saved, the Empire would have recovered the Death Star plans, and the Rebellion would have been crushed. And don't get me started on the poor Ewoks...

"Yes, but": Two words that could destroy the universe.

ALL HEROES EVENTUALLY SAY, "YES, AND"

Star Wars is based on "The Hero's Journey," which is a term coined by Joseph Campbell to refer to a standard story structure found in narratives throughout history from all around the world.

All classic stories follow this structure. In Campbell's own words, in the Hero's Journey, "A hero ventures forth from the world of common day into a region of supernatural wonder: fabulous forces are there encountered and a decisive victory is won: the hero comes back from this mysterious adventure with the power to bestow boons on his fellow man."

The second step in "the Hero's Journey" is "the refusal of the call." The hero is called to adventure, but he refuses. He says, "yes, but" to the call.

Eventually though, the hero gets off his duff and says, "Yes, And," and that's when the journey really gets going.

"The Hero's Journey" is a structure that can be found in stories from every culture around the world. It can be traced back to stories from thousands of years ago. This goes to show two things:

1. Saying "yes, but" is such a natural instinct that it exists in all cultures and has been around forever.

2. All heroes, to become heroes, eventually say "Yes, And."

You may not think of yourself as a hero in the traditional sense. However, consider this: **You are the hero of your own life**. Your life is a story, and you are the main character. You have the choice of being a hero or a bit player. While it sounds depressing to think of yourself as a bit player in the narrative of your own life, this is exactly what you do when you say, "yes, but."

Don't settle. Be the hero of your own story. Say, "Yes, And."

HISTORY RESPECTS "YES, AND"

History is filled with people who faced obstacles and chose to say, "Yes, And" instead of "yes but." In fact, history only remembers (in the positive) people who said "Yes, And" instead of "yes, but."

Bill Gates: *"Yes, And everyone will benefit from having a computer,"* as opposed to "yes, but no one will ever need a home computer" (as several of his contemporaries said).

Gandhi: *"Yes, And we can have our freedom without resorting to violence,"* as opposed to, "yes, but we will never gain our freedom if we don't fight our oppressors!"

Copernicus: *"Yes, And my tests show that the Earth revolves around the sun and not the other way around,"* as opposed to, "yes, but everyone knows that the Earth is the center of the universe!"

"YES, AND" GETS YOU SOMEWHERE, EVEN IF IT'S NOT WHERE YOU PLANNED

One of the best parts of saying "Yes, And" is that it takes you somewhere. It may not be where you originally planned, but at least it is different from where you started.

If you feel stuck, it's easy to say "yes, but" to every option that comes your way. The problem with that is that "yes, but" does nothing but keep you stuck in the same place.

"Yes, And" gets you moving. It gets you unstuck. You may not get to exactly where you originally intended, but you'll be someplace new. That means new options and new possibilities. It also means new momentum.

Of course, you don't want to be stupid about it. However, you will learn more by saying, "Yes, And," taking some action, and getting someplace new than you will by sitting around forever trying to think of the perfect plan.

By simply saying, "Yes, And let's see where this goes," you will start making progress.

"YES, AND" CUSTOMER SERVICE

If there is an obvious business application to saying, "Yes, And," it is in customer service. Every customer service interaction in the world would greatly improve if everyone just kept a "Yes, And" mindset.

Think back to the worst customer service experiences you have had. I would bet that behind every single one of those experiences was a person saying, literally or figuratively, "yes, but."

"Yes, but" seems to have become the default customer service response. "Yes but that's not my job." "Yes but we don't accept returns." "Yes but you are wrong." "Yes but I can't help you."

The silver lining on the customer service gray cloud is that since "yes, but" is so ubiquitous, the people and organizations that use, "Yes, And" will truly stand out for exemplary service.

Which side of the "Yes, And/yes, but" coin do you want to be on? The side that is lauded for amazing service, or the side that gets lambasted for creating horrible experiences?

A REAL LIFE EXAMPLE OF "YES, BUT" AND "YES, AND" CUSTOMER SERVICE

A few years ago I had the unfortunate experience of having a problem with my cable bill. It turns out the cable company thought I had kept one of their cable boxes when I last moved (I didn't) and they were charging me $700 for it.

I called to speak to a representative about this, and the person I spoke with was a classic "yes, butter."

"Yes, but our records show that you still have it. Yes but you are going to have to pay. Yes, but you should have done blah blah blah."

Then, in an act of divine intervention, the battery on my cordless phone died and I was disconnected. At the time I was upset because I was on the middle of a discussion and was trying to make my point. Now I would have to start all over.

I called again from a different phone and was connected with a different representative. Wow, what a difference! It was a 180 degree turnaround.

This second person I spoke to was a wonderful "Yes, And" person. She listened to my story with an open mind, asked me a question or two, then suggested a simple course of action I could take to clear up the matter.

Essentially, the first person told me, "yes, but you're wrong." The second said, "Yes, And to fix the problem here's what you have to do."

Same company, same situation, same day, two very different people.

Who would you rather speak to? Who works at your organization? Who are you in customer service situations?

THE "YES, BUT" SALESPERSON

In sales, "Yes, And" is a way of becoming a partner with your prospect. You don't argue with them or try to strongly convince them of the benefits of your product or service. Instead, you have a conversation with them and help them determine what they truly need.

When an objection is raised in the sales process, your immediate instinct may be to respond with, "yes, but." If the prospect says, "it's too expensive," you may want to say, "yes, but it's cheaper than our competitor's!" If he says, "I don't think I really need it," you may want to say, "yes, but if you just listen to what I am saying you'll see that you do." If she says, "I just want to think about it," you may want to say, "yes, but if you don't decide now you'll never get this price again."

These tactics may close some sales, but you will surely create some buyer's remorse. You also won't be building the rapport that leads to long term relationships, repeat sales, and referrals.

I once met a woman at a networking meeting and it seemed like we might be able to help each other, so we met for lunch. At the meeting, she spent some time asking me about my business, which was nice, but when the conversation turned to her she suddenly went into "presentation mode." I was no longer talking to a person; I felt like I was talking to an infomercial.

At some point she started addressing all of my concerns and objections with "yes, buts." I was so confused by the turn of events I ended up signing up for her service, but I left the meeting with a terrible taste in my mouth. My credit card expired soon after, and I never gave her the updated info. I also never spoke to that woman again, nor did I refer any business to her.

That's the danger of being a "yes, but" sales person. You may win the battle, but you will usually lose the war.

THE "YES, AND" SALESPERSON

The "Yes, And" salesperson takes a different approach. When faced with an objection, rather than setting up an adversarial relationship and immediately arguing back with a "yes, but," she says, "Yes, And" and seeks to understand the prospect's point of view.

For example:

Yes but:

Prospect: This product is too expensive!

Salesperson: Yes, but it's cheaper than comparable brands on the market!

Yes, And:

Prospect: This product is too expensive!

Salesperson: Yes, And I can see that's a concern. Can I show you some products we have that fit into your budget?

Or:

Salesperson: Yes, And that's why we have set up payment plans. Would you be interested in hearing about them?

Or:

Salesperson: Yes, it is expensive, And it will pay for itself in six months with the savings it will provide.

Often, the end result of the sales conversation will be the same as in the "yes, but" conversation. You may still point out the reasons why the prospect doesn't need to worry about their objection. However, by approaching from a "Yes, And" place you:

a) Understand whether the objection is the real issue,

b) Determine whether your solution really is the best thing for them, and

c) Create a connection with the prospect by truly understanding and considering their needs.

This simple shift of saying, "Yes, And" (and having the ensuing conversation) can build wonderful long term relationships that lead to repeat business and lots of referrals.

"YES, AND" TEAMWORK

Can you imagine what your work day would look like if you and everyone around you simply started saying "Yes, And" to each other instead of "yes, but"?

Imagine the positive energy and work environment that would be created, the collaboration that would occur, and the creativity that would be unleashed.

As much time and energy is spent on teambuilding in the corporate world, you would think that this would be an obvious technique occurring already on every level of every organization. But sadly it is not.

All the teambuilding in the world is meaningless if you cannot just get your team to say, "Yes, And" to each other. If you can, then there is nothing that your team cannot accomplish.

"YES, AND" LEADERSHIP

The "Yes, And" leader is a rare find indeed.

Leaders who "Yes, And" their employees (or volunteers. Or followers. Or whoever) realize that their people are their greatest asset. They also realize that while they were surely hired because of their skill, they can still benefit from being open minded and soliciting ideas from others.

"Yes, And" leaders cultivate relationships with their people. If someone comes to them with a crazy idea, they don't cut them off with a "yes, but that will never work." Instead they listen with an open mind. When they ask their team questions, those questions are designed to probe deeper, not to challenge or demonstrate error. "Yes, And" leaders understand that by taking a few moments to listen (really listen, not just pretend to listen while they do five other things) they accomplishes three critical goals:

1. **They build relationships with their employees based on respect.** The simple act of paying attention and considering the idea, even if they disagree with it and "know" it won't work, conveys respect. When, at the end of the conversation, the leader has to say, "We can't do it," the employee will feel like his idea was considered and he was respected. That builds loyalty and an environment of collaboration and teamwork.

2. **They open the door to the possibility of a new idea.** As humans, we like to label things as soon as we see them. When an employee starts talking about an idea, their boss immediately thinks back through his history and tries to match it up with an idea that has already happened. This is what allows the "yes, but" leader to "yes, but" so quickly.

   However, it is possible that the employee is presenting a truly new idea. Or, if it's not a new idea, it may be a new spin on an old idea that just might work. By having an open minded conversation, the "Yes, And" leader opens the door to innovation.

   "Yes, And" leaders accept the possibility that they have people working for them that just may be smarter than they are. In fact, they rely on it.

3. **They contribute to building a "Yes, And" organization.** Consciously or not, we learn from our mentors, our leaders, and our role models. If an employee is constantly "yes, butted," guess what? It won't be long before he becomes a "yes, butter" himself. If, instead, his leader consistently leads with a "Yes, And" approach, he will model that behavior. He will treat others with a "Yes, And" mindset. And when he

becomes a leader himself, he too will be a "Yes, And" leader.

"YES, AND" RELATIONSHIPS

Can "Yes, And" save a marriage? Yes. Yes it can.

I was recording a product of myself teaching the "Yes, And" idea, and my friend Jenn was working the camera. It was the first time she had heard my stuff, and even though she was working the camera and not an actual attendee of my program, she got something out of it.

A few months later I was at a party Jenn was hosting when I hear her call out, "that's the guy!" while pointing at me. I had no idea what this was about, so later on I asked her about it.

Jenn said, "I told my friend who was having marital problems about your 'Yes, And vs. yes, but,' idea. At the party she was chatting with some other friends who were having some issues, and she said to them, 'Oh, we used to have lots of problems too, and we even went to counseling and therapy, and nothing seemed to work. And then Jenn told me about 'Yes, And' and 'yes, but,' and I realized that was our problem. So we switched from being a 'yes, but' couple to being a 'Yes, And' couple and our relationship got better.' At that point I let her know that I got it from you, so I yelled out, 'that's the guy!'"

So simple. "We switched from being a "yes, but" couple to being a "Yes, And" couple and our relationship got better."

If you are in a relationship, what kind of couple are you? If you are not in a romantic relationship, you are still in relationships with friends and family. Are those "Yes, And" or "yes, but" relationships?

"YES, AND" IS WHY YOU ARE HERE

Not to sound too grandiose or spiritual, but you are here on this Earth to say, "Yes, And."

Regardless of what you are doing, you are not here to say, "yes, but."

"Yes, but" is about playing small and limiting yourself. "Yes, And" is how you make the most of your time on this planet.

Said in a different way, "Yes, And" is the reason you are here. If you have an employer, your boss needs you to say, "Yes, And" and get things done. If you have your own business, your customers need you to say, "Yes, And" and solve their problems. If you are in a relationship, your partner needs you to say, "Yes, And" and help the relationship grow and flourish. If you are a parent, your children need you to say, "Yes, And" and help them develop and fulfill their potential.

You are not put into situations to say, "yes, but." You are put into situations to find ways to say, "Yes, And."

"YES, AND" IS PERSISTENCE. "YES, BUT" IS EXCUSES.

When you choose to say, "yes, but," you are letting yourself off the hook with an excuse. 99% of the time whatever follows the "yes, but" is an excuse. This is not to say that all excuses are negative; some are valid. But regardless of the validity, saying "yes, but" is giving yourself the easy way out.

"Yes, And" is the language of persistence. You are saying, "Yes, this happened, And here is what I am going to do about it."

Here's the thing: Persistence is hard. Saying, "Yes, And" is hard. It is so much easier to say, "yes, but," make an excuse, and go on your merry way. Unfortunately, all growth, progress, and success comes from being persistent. It is hard, but it is worth doing.

If you condition yourself to think and act "Yes, And" you will set yourself up to persist and persevere in the face of adversity. And that's a good thing because guess what? No matter what you are trying to accomplish, if it is worth doing you will face adversity. "Yes, And" will help you push past it.

"YES, AND" AND THE DIP

In his marvelous little book, "The Dip," Seth Godin explains how all great success comes from pushing through "the Dip." The Dip is the point when the going gets tough. Most people won't persevere and push through the Dip. They give up too soon. This is quite sad, because on the other side of the Dip is where the real rewards lie.

"Yes, And" gets you through the Dip. When you find yourself in a Dip, say, "Yes, And" and take the forward action to get through it. It will be well worth it – according to Seth (and me!)

THE FEAR OF SAYING "YES, AND"

It can be a bit scary to say "Yes, And." Scratch that; it can be downright terrifying!

When you say "Yes, And" you thrust yourself into the great unknown. You are out of your comfort zone, out of your area of expertise, and out of what you know to be good and safe.

As humans, we fear the unknown. And we fear change. The brain likes familiarity. It likes everything to stay just as it is.

So if you feel trepidation (or downright panic) when you think about saying, "Yes, And," realize that you are not alone. That is a natural response that everyone feels. The trick is to not be paralyzed by it. As Susan Jeffers says in her best-selling book of the same name, "feel the fear and do it anyway!"

SAYING "YES, BUT" OUT OF FEAR IS A LOUSY WAY TO LIVE

Have you ever backed away from a confrontation, an argument, a fight, or from doing the right thing out of fear? How does it feel afterward? Not good, right?

Even if backing down is the right thing (as it usually is when it comes to physical violence) you feel bad afterward. The "coulda, shoulda, wouldas" come out in force.

That's what it feels like to let fear dictate your actions.

It's one thing to make a sensible decision based on weighing the possibilities of risk and reward. It's another to reflexively say, "yes, but" out of fear.

When you repeatedly say, "yes, but" out of fear, you are setting yourself up to feel those pangs of regret, those negative feelings, those "coulda, shoulda, wouldas" over and over and over again. And that can be a pretty lousy way to live.

Saying, "Yes, And" takes a little courage, but isn't that the way you would prefer to live your life anyway?

DON'T BE AN IDIOT

When you start thinking about saying "Yes, And" in the face of fear, it's easy to put your attention on the extreme cases:

"What if you're trying to decide whether you should go bungee jumping off a cliff with an unlicensed operator?? Are you saying I should say, 'Yes, And' to that?!?"

No, of course not. What I am saying is that when your friend comes to you and says, "Want to go bungee jumping?" don't say, "no way!" right out of hand.

Think about how you can say, "Yes, And." Then if you think you might like to stretch yourself, do your research and make a smart and informed decision.

Remember, the goal is not to blindly say, "Yes, And" to everything without any thought. The goal is to change your default reaction so you can use "Yes, And" as a tool to grow, find and seize opportunities, and take your life to the next level.

"Yes, And" is about making smart decisions based on seeing and considering all your options.

To summarize: Don't be an idiot, and you'll be fine using, "Yes, And."

WHAT HAS SAYING "YES, BUT" COST YOU?

You don't need me to regale you with story after story of people who have shortchanged themselves by saying "yes, but" to opportunities that have come their way. I would guess that all you need to do is to think back over your own life and you will be able to find examples of many times you said "yes, but" and settled for less than you deserved.

What has "yes, but" cost you? What is it still costing you today? Think back over the things you regret in life. Sure, some of them will be regrets such as, "I wish I had not said that mean thing," but most of them will be regrets about saying, "yes, but." "I wish I had taken a chance and applied to grad school (instead of saying, "yes but I'll never get in)." "I regret not asking out my best friend from college who I had a crush on (instead of saying, "yes, but she will probably reject me)." "I regret not going out on my own and starting my own business like I wanted (instead of saying, "yes, but my business would probably fail)."

We most often regret the things we don't do. "Yes, but" is the two word recipe to never do anything, never try anything, and never attempt anything. Simply put, "yes, but" is the two word recipe to lead a life filled with regrets.

Take a second and ask yourself, "what has yes but been costing me?"

YOU SHOULD BE ANGRY

Does this make you angry? Good, you should be angry.

But don't be angry at me, I'm just the messenger. Besides, I have enough to deal with trying to manage my own inner desires

For a special free gift, exclusively for book owners, visit: www.SayYesAnd.com/bookgift

to say, "yes, but."

Don't be too angry at yourself either. There is nothing wrong with you. You're not broken or messed up. Saying "yes, but" is a natural tendency that everyone falls into. Give yourself a break and don't beat yourself up over it.

On the other hand, don't let yourself completely off the hook. If you are unhappy with where you are in your career (or business. Or relationships. Or activities. Or wherever) chances are you mostly have your own "yes, buts" to blame. If you are truly honest with yourself and dig deep you'll find a list of "yes, buts" you have been telling yourself that have been holding you back.

Take a moment to think about that and get a little angry at yourself. Realize that it's not the other people in the world, or your circumstances, or your bad luck. It's just all the times you have said, "yes, but" instead of "Yes, And" that are limiting you.

This may sound negative and depressing, but it's quite the opposite. Once you realize that your own, "yes, buts" are the problem, you also realize that you hold the key to your own solution. Start adding more "Yes, And" into your life and you will find yourself taking charge of your own life and moving closer to what you want.

So be angry for a little bit. Then let go of that anger, say, "Yes, And," and start doing something about it.

"YES AND," PUTS YOU IN THE DRIVER'S SEAT

"Yes, but" is a very passive way to live. The "but" is often seen as something outside of yourself.

"Yes, but they messed up. Yes, but my competition had an inside connection. Yes, but an unexpected storm delayed my flight."

And when the "yes, but" focus does shift from someone or something else onto yourself, it comes in the form of giving up.

"Yes, but I'm not good enough. Yes, but I'm not qualified. Yes, but I can't."

The running theme in all of these "yes, buts" is the idea of control. More correctly, it's the lack of control.

"Yes, but" is a way of complaining about something and framing the problem in a way where you have no control. Your ego likes this; it means it's not your fault!

"Yes, And" puts you back where you belong: in the driver's seat.

If the problem is truly external to you, you say, "Yes, this is what happened, And here is what I am going to do about it."

If the problem is internal to you, you say, "Yes, I currently have this limitation, And here is what I am going to do about it."

Notice the theme? "Yes, And" puts the focus on what you are going to do.

The next time you encounter a problem and you feel the urge to blame someone else, try saying, "Yes, And here's what I'm going to do about it." You'll feel better, and react much more effectively – even if it really was someone else's fault.

BE A SUPERSTAR BY SAYING "YES, AND"

"Yes, And" people are superstars. They are superstars at work. They are superstars in their associations and community groups. They are superstars to their friends and family.

Why is that? Because by saying, "Yes, And" instead of "yes, but" they become the "Go-To Guy" (or girl).

Think about your own life: who are the superstars?

- It is the friend who, whenever you are in a pickle, you can ask for their help and they will say, "Yes, And I am here for you."
- It is the colleague who, when you have an important project that you need a homerun effort on, you know will say, "Yes, And I will go the extra mile for you."

- It is the vendor who, when you need a rush order on a special request, will say, "Yes, And we'll figure out a way of making this work for you."

In short, it is the person who, no matter what you go to them with, will say, "Yes, And I will help you."

Be a superstar. Be the Go-to-Guy. Say, "Yes, And."

RELIABILITY AND CONSISTENCY

What we are talking about here is reliability. People become superstars because they are reliable. No matter what is asked of them, they will come through for you (or your team, association, or company).

Saying, "Yes, And" is how you get the reputation for reliability. That is how you become the superstar.

The key is that you have to say, "Yes, And" consistently. You can't just say it once, and assume word will spread. You can't say it sometimes, and hope that people remember your "Ands" more than your "buts."

Of course, after you say, "Yes, And" you have to deliver on what you promise. Saying, "Yes, And" and dropping the ball is a good way to destroy your reputation. If you plan on doing that, you are much better off just saying, "yes, but."

"YES, AND" AND BOUNDARY ISSUES

At this point, I know what you are thinking: "If I start saying "Yes, And" to every request I will be overwhelmed! I will not have enough time to do everything. Worst of all, since I will be stretched too thin I will drop the ball on the stuff I said, "Yes, And" to and that will make me look worse than just saying, "yes, but" in the first place!"

You have a point. No one said this would be easy...

While it's true that you cannot agree to do everything that

comes your way, you should not use that as an excuse to avoid saying, "Yes, And." Here are ways to say "Yes, And" without drowning in activity.

1. **Prioritize** — First off, you should prioritize your "Yes, And" activities. You don't need to be a superstar to everyone in every situation. In fact you can't be. Perhaps you want to be a superstar in your job, but are happy to be a solid role player for your professional associations. Maybe you want to be a superstar to your spouse and children but just a good family member to your extended family. You might have a tight circle of friends to whom you are a superstar, but a wider network of acquaintances who you simply help as you can.

   Of course, the more areas you are a superstar in and the more people who consider you a superstar, the better. You never know where your next opportunity will come from. The more people who see you as the reliable "Go-To-Guy," the more people who can love, hire, promote, and reward you.

   Keep in mind however, that the goal is to become a "Yes, And" person. The goal is to make saying, "Yes, And" a reflex. You'll find yourself thinking "Yes, And" to every opportunity, and then, after thinking things through and prioritizing, saying, "yes, but" to opportunities you need to pass on.

2. **Dig Deeper** — If you are stretched too thin to say, "Yes, And" to a friend's request, you still don't have to say, "yes, but" out of hand. Have a "Yes, And" conversation with her to see if a) there is a way you can still help or b) you can help her figure out some other ways to achieve her goal.

   If you are asked to take on a project that you don't think you will be able to handle because of time, don't just say, "No thank you." (Or, "no way!!"). Instead, try a few moments of "Yes, And." "Yes, And what does this project entail?" "Yes, And why do you need this project done?" "Yes, And is there another way of achieving that same goal?"

3. Redirect — When someone approaches you with a request, you assume that there are only two options: "yes" and "no." "Yes, And" can allow you to redirect to a third option.

This is one of those areas where you can turn a literal, "no," into a powerful "Yes, And." If someone wants you to chair a committee for your association but you truly feel you do not have the time to do it properly, you can respond with, "I don't have the time to take on that position, but here are some ways I would be happy to help." Or, "that is a little out of what I feel comfortable doing, but is there a smaller role I can help with?" Or even, "I have to pass, but here are some suggestions for who would be great in this role."

A simple redirect takes that focus off of what you can't do and on to what you can.

4. Change the language, change the energy — Sometimes you can say the exact same thing and just switch "but" to "and" and you will create a completely different energy.

For example, when discussing a project, you might be tempted to say, "Yes, I can do that for you, but I can not get to it until next week." The exact same statement rephrased with an "and" would be, "Yes, I can do that for you, And I can start as soon as next week."

In the "but" version you are setting up a negative energy. You are expressing your answer in a way that assumes disappointment.

In the "And" version, you set up a positive energy. It almost sounds like you are doing them a favor by starting next week!

The goal here is not to mislead or manipulate. However, once you become a "Yes, And" person you will start thinking about things in a more positive light. By switching one word and making your response more positive, you completely change the energy and dynamic from adversarial to cooperative.

5. Stretch Yourself! — Of course, one of the best things you can do is to just say, "Yes, And" to yourself and accept some of the extra responsibility, even if you feel it will be a bit of a stretch.

There is nothing wrong with stretching yourself! That is how you grow. You are also probably capable of accomplishing a lot more than you give yourself credit for (i.e. you have been "yes, butting" you own assessment of your ability to get things done).

I have come across more than a few people who have let great opportunities to become superstars pass them by because they were afraid to say, "Yes, And" and stretch themselves. Don't be afraid! A little pressure can be a good thing. Stretch yourself, say, "Yes, And," and do a great job. That is the first step to superstardom!

Remember, "Yes, And" is a mentality. The point is not for you to stretch yourself so thin doing other people's work that you burn yourself out. The goal is to simply make you the person people go to first, so you can be the true superstar.

FEAR, POSSIBILITY, AND "YES, AND"

WHY WE DON'T SAY "YES, AND"

If saying "Yes, And" is so super, why don't we always do it?

Put simply, it's because saying "Yes, And" is hard. Saying "yes, but" is much, much easier.

"Yes, And" gets you off the couch and into the gym. "Yes, but" lets you order another round of beer and nachos.

"Yes, And" makes you have that important conversation you want to avoid. "Yes, but" lets you avoid it.

"Yes, And" forces you to pursue that idea, take that class, or start that business you have been thinking about. "Yes, but" lets you put it off until next year.

"Yes, And" wants you to jump on opportunities that come your way. "Yes, but" lets you come up with excuses to let them pass you by.

"Yes, And" requires you to get creative, challenge assumptions, and think of new options. "Yes, but" lets you keep doing things the same way you always have (regardless of whether that's a good thing).

"Yes, And" is the road less travelled. "Yes, but" is not a road at all; it's a dead end.

"Yes, And" **forces** you into action, "yes, but" **lets** you sit on your duff.

"Yes, And" is a lot scarier than "yes, but," but it's also a lot more exciting and productive.

WHEN IT'S OK TO SAY "YES, BUT"

It is important to note that saying, "yes, but" is not necessarily a bad thing. I am sure after reading this you feel that, "yes, but" is the root of all evil. However, it is perfectly acceptable to say, "yes, but" if you have first looked for a way to say, "Yes, And."

No one is telling you to do anything and everything people tell you to. That is a recipe for disaster! However, you should consider doing what people ask you to. Rather than "yes, butting" it out of hand, think "Yes, And" first. Give some weight to what is being said. Be open minded. Take a moment and explore the idea.

Then, once you have mulled over the idea with a fully open "Yes, And" mindset, it is perfectly acceptable for you to say, "yes, but this won't work for me and here's why."

DON'T FOOL YOURSELF

Don't fool yourself. Many people will read the previous section about saying, "yes, but" and assume that all the times they say, "yes, but" they are being open minded. If that was true, the world would be a much more pleasant place.

Err on the side of over "Yes Anding," especially at first.

Consciously think "Yes, And." Actually hear yourself saying the words (in your own head). Over time it will become automatic. When it does, then you can be somewhat confident that when you say "yes, but" you are doing so with an open-minded and respectful approach.

BLASTING LIMITED THINKING

"Yes, And" blasts away limited thinking. "Yes, but" is the language of limitations, constraints, and complacency. For example, here are some "yes, but" responses to the thought, "I would love to do that..."

- "Yes but I am not good enough."
- "Yes but I don't have the funds."
- "Yes but no one will pay me for that."

These all represent limited thinking.

On the other hand, it is close to impossible to think small when you say, "Yes, And." For example, imagine you think to yourself, "I should start a business." When you apply "Yes, And" to it:

- "Yes, And that would let me do what I love."
- "Yes, And that would make me happy, which would spill into other areas of my life."
- "Yes, And then I would have better relationships with my spouse and family."
- "Yes, And that would make me even more productive."
- "Yes, And then I would make more money."
- "Yes, And then I could grow my business and take on staff to expand and grow."
- "Yes, And then I could franchise or license my business model and start letting other people make money for me."
- "Yes, And then I could sell the business for millions of dollars and never have to worry about money again."
- "Yes, And...Yes, And...Yes, And..."

Are you guaranteed that just by saying, "Yes, And" that you will automatically build a successful multimillion dollar business? Of course not. But you can be guaranteed that saying, "yes, but" will stop you before you even get out of the gate. For example "I should start a business":

- "Yes, but it might not work."
- "Yes, but I might lose a lot of money."
- "Yes, but it's too risky."
- "Yes, but I am better off staying at my current job, even though I don't like it."

BLASTING OTHER PEOPLE'S LIMITED THINKING

If someone you know (a friend, colleague, family member, etc.) comes to you with a grand idea, is your first response to say, "yes, but" or "Yes, And"?

If it's "yes, but," then you are contributing to their limited thinking. You are helping them live a life well below their potential.

Simply by saying, "Yes, And" to them, you can help them blast their own limited thinking. You don't need to be a motivational speaker, or a cheerleader, or a success coach. You just need to say "Yes, And."

So when your buddy comes to you and says, "I am thinking about opening a bakery," you can say, "Yes, And what kind of baked goods do you want to make?" A simple "Yes, And" response will stoke the creative fires and build motivation all by itself.

BE WARY OF GOOD INTENTIONS

It is quite possible that your friend has no business baking a tin of cupcakes, much less opening his own bakery. Maybe he can't cook. Maybe he has no business sense. Or maybe he comes up with a new idea every week and never actually follows through on them. Should you still say, "Yes, And" and encourage him even if you think it is a stupid idea and doomed to fail?

Perhaps not. You might be better off giving him some guidance and advice, or helping him indentify what his real goal is and then helping him create a real plan to achieve that goal. However, saying, "no" or "yes, but" is not the best way to do this.

Often times when you say, "yes, but," you have good intentions. "I'd better point out to him how stupid this idea is before he throws away any money on it."

However, just because your motives are pure, that doesn't mean your implementation is sound. There are ways of protecting people from danger without crushing their spirit. In fact, "Yes, And" allows you to redirect them so you can take their passion and enthusiasm and help them channel it down a better path.

To do this you have to say, "Yes, And." You can't say to your baker friend, "yes, but you should open a different business because you can't bake!" (even though that may be true). That will either

1) Make him feel dejected or
2) Make him defiant so he redoubles his commitment down the bad path "just to show you!"

"Yes, And" allows you to dig deeper and gently redirect if needed. To your baker friend, you could say, "Yes, And why is it that you want to be a baker?" "Oh, you love the idea of waking up and making people happy in the morning. Yes, And what is it about that that you like?" "Ah, you are a morning person and a people person, and baking reminds you of your grandmother. Yes, And are there other ways you can interact with people in the morning and still honor your grandmother that don't require baking?"

Too often, people just want to "say their peace." That way if things go wrong, they can always say, "I told you so," or, "I tried to talk you out of it." If that is your motive, then you are not really interested in trying to help the other person, you are just interested in not looking bad yourself if things go wrong. That's what people in the corporate world call "CYA." (Cover Your A__)

Intentions aren't enough. If you really care about helping people avoid danger and get on a better path, you need to speak to them in a way that gets them on board. "Yes, And" lets you do that.

IF IT'S WORTH DOING, IT'S OUT OF YOUR COMFORT ZONE

Right now, you have a "comfort zone." We all do. You also probably have some goals or dreams. Here's the thing: If you want to achieve those dreams, you're going to have to get out of your comfort zone.

I know what you're thinking: "Why would I want to do that? My comfort zone is so darned comfortable, after all!"

And you are right. It is comfortable in there. However, there's one simple reason you need to get out of your comfort zone: because that is where all of your progress, growth, and success lies.

Think about it: if the ability to attain all you want is within your comfort zone, you would already have those things. Ergo, if there are things in life that you want, things in life that you would like to change, dreams that you would like to achieve, and you are not currently on the path to get them, then you need to get

For a special free gift, exclusively for book owners, visit: www.SayYesAnd.com/bookgift

out of your comfort zone.

Even if you are already on the path, that path can change. It can take a serious detour. And it can end. When that happens, will you say, "yes, but I was on the path!" and give up? Or will you say, "Yes, And here is what happened, let me take a step in a new direction"?

When you say "yes, but" you are in essence stepping up to the edge of your comfort zone and saying, "yes, I could step out, but instead I will stay right here." A more powerful way is to say, "Yes, I could step out, And I will now take that step."

Remember, if it's worth doing, it's out of your comfort zone. And that means you need to say, "Yes, And."

YOU MUST KEEP, "YES, ANDING" YOUR COMFORT ZONE

You may think that you can simply say, "Yes, And" once, expand your comfort zone, and be done with it. Sorry, it doesn't work that way.

Your goal is not to expand your comfort zone once and be done with it. Your goal is to develop a mindset where you continuously expand your comfort zone and open yourself up to greater growth and progress. That's what, "Yes, And" will do for you.

Once you have expanded your comfort zone, great! But guess what? Now you have a new comfort zone. Enjoy it for what it is, but realize that at some point (the sooner the better) the new zone won't be enough. You'll have to "Yes, And" it again. Then you'll have to do it again. And again. And again…

"YES, AND" ISN'T ABOUT CONSTANT STRIVING

This idea may sound depressing, as if you'll never be satisfied with what you have, but it isn't.

Saying, "Yes, And" is all about being satisfied with what you have. "Yes, but" is about striving – "yes, I have this, but I need more." That creates a sense of desperation and unhappiness.

"Yes, And" allows you to appreciate what you have while keeping you in a state of continual growth. "Yes, I have this, And I will keep making progress towards something more."

Constant progress is a good thing. Adopting a "Yes, And" mindset automatically keeps you on that path.

USING "YES, AND" TO REDUCE STRESS

Having the "Yes, And" mindset is an excellent way to reduce stress.

One major cause of stress is obsessing about possible future consequences.

For example, when the economy is bad, people stress about losing their jobs. Underneath all that stress is a "yes, but" mindset.

"Yes, but if I lose my job I won't be able to pay my bills!"

"Yes, but if I lose my job I won't be able to find another one!"

"Yes, but if I lose my job I'll be a loser!"

The "Yes, And" approach to stress reduction is to simply say, "Yes, And if I lose my job, I'll deal with it."

I had a friend who had to move out of her apartment, and she couldn't find a moving company. Everyone she called was booked solid. This led to some serious stress as she thought, "yes, but what if I can't find a moving company!?!"

My response was to say, "If that happens, we'll deal with it."

And we would have. It may have sucked. We may have had to do the entire move with just the two of us, which would have

For a special free gift, exclusively for book owners, visit: www.SayYesAnd.com/bookgift

been a long, painful day (perhaps spilling into the next night). We could have had to pay a super high premium to convince some company to take the job. We may have had to hire a bunch of uninsured people from Craigslist for the move and potentially had stuff get lost or broken.

All of those things would have sucked. But we would have dealt with it.

You may be thinking, "But that's stupid! All those scenarios are awful! How is that "dealing with it"?"

Because it is dealing with it. "Dealing with it" simply means that you will take it as it comes and do your best. You might deal with it very adeptly, or you might deal with it terribly. But at the end of the day, you will deal with it.

The key is to realize that saying, "yes, but," and stressing out accomplish nothing! All that does is ruin your quality of life for the days, weeks, or even months leading up to the event you are dreading. Saying, "Yes, And" at least allows you to let go of that stress and accept the fact that yes, no matter what happens, you will deal with it!

Of course a little preparation goes a long way towards making sure you have fewer things to deal with. And if you are having a problem, saying, "yes, but" and stressing and complaining will make you feel overwhelmed and paralyzed. Saying, "Yes, And" will allow you to let the stress go and refocus on doing what you can now to fix the problem.

And as for my friend's move? We found movers in advance and everything went fine. All that, "yes, but" stress was for nothing.

ES, AND" AND DEALING WITH THE UNEXPECTED

When unexpected setbacks happen (as they always do) you have a choice: you can say, "Yes, And" or "yes, but." If you want to flow with the unexpected effectively, you must choose, "Yes, And."

"Yes, but" is whining. "Yes, but this wasn't supposed to happen! Yes, but if you had just done what I suggested we wouldn't be in this situation! Yes, but I don't know what to do now!""

"Yes, And" is the language of acceptance and action. "Yes, this has happened, And here is what I am going to do about it. Yes, And let's take care of what we can with what we have. Yes, And let's make the best of a bad situation."

"YES, AND" IS HOW YOU GET LUCKY

No, not that kind of lucky. Get your mind out of the gutter.

I'm talking about the kind of luck that some people just seem to have. They happen to sit next to a person on a flight and that conversation leads to a lucrative business partnership. They get selected from a huge pool of applicants to participate in an exclusive internship. They have a chance encounter with someone at a networking event who goes on to be a mentor, benefactor, investor, or even a romantic interest.

You know those people. They are the people that make the rest of us jealous.

Here's the thing: those people aren't actually any luckier than you or me. They just say, "Yes, And" a whole lot more.

The person on the plane? She said, "Yes, And" to having a conversation, when so many of us would have said, "yes, but what if the person is boring," or, "yes, but I just want to sleep." She probably had many such "Yes, And" conversations that led nowhere, but they set her up for the one that mattered.

The one who got selected for the exclusive program? He said, "Yes, And" to applying, instead of, "yes, but I won't get selected." He also said "Yes, And" many times leading up to that application, building his experience, credentials, and skill set so that he would be a more enticing candidate.

The person with the chance encounter at the networking event? She said, "Yes, And" to attending that event, as she probably had to dozens or hundreds before. She also said, "Yes, And" to that conversation, and "Yes, And" to following up.

If you want a little more luck in your life, forget about rabbit's feet, horseshoes, and four-leafed clovers. Just start saying "Yes, And" a whole lot more.

"YES, AND" INNOVATION

"Yes, And" is the attitude at the heart of innovation.

The dictionary defines innovation as, "a new method, idea, or device." The operative word in that definition is "new."

You can not innovate with "yes, but," because "yes, but," by its very nature blocks you from moving into anything new.

In this day and age, companies as large as the Fortune 100 and as small as one-person shops need to innovate to stay competitive in an ever-changing market. If you, or the members of your team or organization, are locked into "yes, but" thinking, you will never innovate. You will never change. You will be left behind by other faster, nimbler, more flexible competitors who are willing to say, "Yes, And."

If innovation matters to you (as it should), then you'll adopt a "Yes, And" attitude. Otherwise, you may as well just run up the white flag.

THE OSTRICH IS A "YES, BUTTER"

People suffer from the illusion that if they are stressing about something, they are somehow "handling it." Nothing could be further from the truth.

Saying, "yes, but" to a bad (or potentially bad) situation is just a way of avoiding it. You are sticking your head in the sand and saying, "yes, but this wasn't supposed to happen."

When you do that, nothing gets solved, nothing gets fixed, and nothing gets improved.

Don't be an ostrich. When disaster strikes, say, "Yes, And," face the problem, and fix it.

NOTHING HAPPENS UNTIL YOU SAY "YES, AND"

"Yes, but" is also the language of paralysis. It is the language of denial. "Yes, butters" avoid problems, using their, "but" to focus on everything but what matters: the actions they can take right now to make things better.

Nothing happens until you say, "Yes, And." Once you do, you have moved from focusing on the problem to focusing on the solution. From complaining to talking about options. From paralysis to action.

Don't be an ostrich. When disaster strikes, say, "Yes, And" and face it and fix it.

THE "YES, AND" ATTITUDE

Those two simple words, "Yes, And" are the key to maintaining a positive attitude. Not only do you have to be more positive to say, "Yes, And," but also the act of saying it puts you in a more positive mindset.

On the flip side, negative people say, "yes, but." Each subsequent "yes, but" you say makes your attitude worse.

Pay attention to the positive and negative people around you. I guarantee that you'll quickly notice that the positive people are "Yes, Anders" and the negative ones are "yes, butters."

I am not one of those people who believes that a positive attitude is the key to all success in life. It can, however, make you more productive, more creative, and a better teammate and leader. Besides, who wants to go through life miserable?

Say "Yes, And" and spread the good vibes around.

AVOIDING CONFLICT WITH "YES, AND"

This section is about conflict resolution because proper use of "Yes, And" can get you out of tough situations before they start.

"Yes, but" is the language of an argument. If you are mad at me and I say, "yes, but" I will achieve two things:

1) I will stay opposed to you.

2) I will make you angrier.

These are two great ways to prolong and escalate a conflict.

When you say, "Yes, And" (and mean it) you are switching from opposition to collaboration. From escalation to resolution. From arguing to understanding.

The next time you sense an argument is about to start, pay careful attention to your desire to say, "yes, but." Before you open your mouth, switch to "Yes, And" and avoid the battle before it begins.

As Mr. Miyagi said, "best defense: no be there."

DON'T BE A PUSHOVER

The natural fear when it comes to saying, "Yes, And" is that you will become a pushover. Rather than sticking to what you believe you will just go along and give in to whatever anyone else suggests.

Though the fear is natural, it is unfounded. You don't have to be a pushover if you say, "Yes, And."

If you only say, "yes," then that makes you a bit of a pushover. It's the "And" that holds the magic.

The "And" is where you have your chance to add your thoughts, share your opinions, and stand by your beliefs. By using "And," you incorporate your ideas and opinions in with the ones provided by others.

Of course there are limits. If you are allergic to shellfish and a friend demands that you go to "Joe's Shrimp Crib" for dinner, you don't have to pull out the Epi-pen. You can decline the shrimp, but rather than saying, "yes, but I'll die you insensitive jerk!" you can say, "Yes, And where else can we go where you can get shrimp and I can eat something too?"

Being skilled in the art of redirection is not about being a pushover. It's about being one of those rare people who helps others get what they want while still getting what you want.

LIVING
A "YES, AND" LIFE

NO ONE IS UNIVERSALLY A "YES, AND" OR "YES, BUT" PERSON

It would be easy to categorize all people as either "Yes, Anders" or "yes, butters." However, it's not that easy.

We are all both "Yes, Anders" and "yes, butters." In some environments you reflexively say, "Yes, And" and in some you reflexively say, "yes, but."

Of course the goal is to say, "Yes, And" reflexively in as many environments as possible.

To start though, pick the areas that are the most important to you. It could be in your business with your customers or co-workers. It could be in your relationships (remember the couple that saved their marriage?). It could be with yourself, in how you limit yourself in pursuing what's important to you.

Start with one area, and make it automatic. Then move on to the next. Then the next. And so on and so on.

You may never completely eliminate saying, "yes, but," but you will certainly make it a rare occurrence.

THE GOAL IS TO MAKE "YES, AND" A DEFAULT REACTION

You may find it hard to say, "Yes, And" at first. If your default response for your whole life has been "yes, but" (or if you have always stayed neutral) it may seem very unnatural to become a "Yes, And" person.

This is how learning happens. Your goal is to make saying and thinking "Yes, And" your default reaction. This doesn't mean you will agree to everything. It just means that your first instinct will be to say, "Yes, And."

In essence, you will be building a habit. The process of habit-building takes four steps:

Step 1 is catching yourself after the fact. You will be in a situation, have a "yes, but" response, and then, later on, realize what you did. Don't beat yourself up when this happens; the simple fact that you noticed is a good thing. It's also the first step in making it a habit. The more you do this, the more the time between you saying "yes, but" and realizing you said it will diminish.

Step 2 is catching yourself as you are doing it. You say "yes, but" and as the words are coming out of your mouth you realize what you are doing. You don't change it; you just notice it as it happens.

Step 3 is thinking about saying "Yes, And" before you respond. You may or may not choose to say, "Yes, And" (you're still learning) but at this point you are consciously aware of whether you are saying "And" or "but."

Step 4 is saying and thinking "Yes, And" as a default response. You may slip into Step 4 without realizing. One day you will encounter a situation, say, "Yes, And" without thinking about it, and then, a few hours later reflect back and realize what you did. At this point you will have built the habit of saying, "Yes, And." At this point you will be a "Yes, And" person.

ACT ON YOUR "YES, AND" BEFORE YOU HAVE A CHANCE TO SAY, "YES, BUT"

If you truly want to live a "Yes, And" life, you need to take action on your "Yes, Ands." Especially when it comes to the "Yes, Ands" and "yes, buts" you say to yourself.

When you start saying, "Yes, And" to yourself, you'll be excited ant motivated to take action. However, being excited and motivated doesn't mean that you will actually do anything about it. You just may sit there and think about taking action on your "Yes, And."

Sadly, the longer you wait to take action, the more time your mind has to start formulating a "yes, but" to talk you out of doing anything. Once the "yes, buts" start, it's hard to quiet them back down.

Don't give your mind a chance to say, "yes, but!" When an idea pops into your head and you find yourself saying, "Yes, And," take action! Do something – anything – to act on your positive "Yes, And" impulse.

I recently heard author, speaker, and radio and television personality Mel Robbins give a talk at a TEDx conference. In her talk, she refers to "the 5-second rule." The 5-second rule states that if you don't act on an idea that pops into your mind within 5 seconds, the idea disappears.

I don't know if this idea is backed up by scientific research, but I know from my own personal experience that it's true. If you think about your own life, you'll probably see that it is true for you as well.

Apply the 5-second rule to your own life. Take action on your "Yes , Ands" before the "yes, buts" have a chance to rear their ugly heads.

ANTICIPATE THE CHALLENGES

"Yes, And" is a concept from the world of improvisational comedy, but that doesn't mean that you can't use a little anticipation and preparation.

You probably know what some of your key, "yes, but" moments are. Maybe there's a certain person that always brings out your "buts." Maybe there is a group you are associated with that brings up your negative side. Maybe it's a certain type of request that makes you say, "yes, but" every time.

If you know what they are in advance, you can prepare for them. If you know that during brainstorming sessions you are the consummate "yes, butter," then before the next session remind yourself to say, "Yes, And." Put a "Yes, And" sticky note on your pad as a constant reminder. Visualize yourself in the meeting saying, "Yes, And"

Whatever works for you, just do it. A little preparation goes a long way.

SAYING "YES, AND" TO A "YES, BUTTER"

Ok, you've seen the light! You have decided that "Yes, And" is the way to go. You start thinking "Yes, And." You start saying, "Yes, And." However, since the people around may not be "Yes, And" people (if not, why haven't you given them this book yet?) your "Yes, Ands" are constantly met with "Yes, Buts."

This is a common problem. "Yes, Anding" a "yes, butter," can be a challenge, but it is doable.

Here are a few things to keep in mind:

1. **You can not take on a hard-core "yes butter" head-on.** Chances are they are more skilled and experienced at saying, "yes, but" than you are at navigating around it with "Yes, And." Besides, one reason saying, "yes, but" is easy is that you don't

have to listen or consider the other person's argument when you say, "yes, but." You can come up with the most brilliant argument for your case ever, and the other person can still say, "yes, but." It's infuriating, and it's why you can't take a "yes, butter" on head-on.

2. **You need to practice redirecting with "Yes, And."** "Yes, Anding" a "yes, butter" is one of the more challenging things you can do. Don't attempt it right out of the gate! You need to practice and get skilled in the art of redirecting with "Yes, And."

3. **The "yes, butter" wants something; Find out what that is.** The "yes, butter" is so adamantly saying, "yes, but" because they, like everyone, want something. That something may or may not be what they are articulating. Re-read the section on, "'Yes, And' Lets You Dig Deeper." That process is even more important with the "yes, butters." You need to use your "Yes, And" skills to redirect around their "buts," dig deeper, and help them get what they want in a different way.

4. **At some point, you'll have to move on.** Remember, one of the main principles in this book is that it's not bad to say, "yes, but." You just need to have a "Yes, And" conversation first. If you are up against a completely stubborn "yes, butter" and are making no headway, and you have legitimately tried to say, "Yes, And" and failed, then drop into your own "yes, but" and move on. It's not a perfect solution, but some fights aren't worth fighting (or if it is worth fighting, you'll have to do it from a "yes, but" place). These situations should be few and far between.

BUILDING A "YES, AND" ORGANIZATION

"YES, AND" AT WORK

"Yes And" is a wonderful way to live, and it can help you achieve greater levels of success. It is a wonderful tool for individual success and progress.

However, where "Yes, And" really comes alive is when you get a group of people all working together and saying "Yes, And" to each other.

Can you imagine what your organization would look like if you and everyone around you said, "Yes, And" instead of "yes, but"?

What would that do to morale? To service? To teamwork? To innovation? To sales? To loyalty?

It's not always going to be easy (heck, it's not usually going to be easy), but it's well worth the effort.

WITH YOUR EMPLOYEES

Creating a "Yes, And" team or organization is easiest when you're the boss, because you can simply demand that people start to say, "Yes, And" instead of "yes, but."

However, change by dictate rarely lasts. If you want to build a "Yes, And" group not just in name, but in spirit and action, there are a few things you should do:

1. **Get your team involved.** It's not enough for you to believe and know that "Yes, And" is a powerful approach to business and life. Your team must also believe it. The easiest way to do that

is not to explain it to them and demand they believe it, but rather to get them involved in the process.

You will of course have to introduce them to the concept. But before you send them back to their jobs expecting them to say, "Yes, And," open a dialog with them. Get their thoughts on whether they even believe that "Yes, And" will work (some are sure to be resistant). Ask them what their questions and concerns are. See what they think the challenges of implementing "Yes, And" will be.

Once you get people involved they take ownership, and that's when change happens.

2. **Start small.** As powerful as, "Yes, And," is, you don't want to try to switch everything over to it all at once. Start with one group, or with one specific job function. Or perhaps start internally, and establish a "Yes, And" rule for brainstorming meetings.

3. **Keep a "Yes, And" Mindset as You Create a "Yes, And" Organization**. You may have a clear vision of what a "Yes, And" organization will look like. Guess what? Some of the other people in your group may have a different idea what that will look like. If you block their input to help you build a "Yes, And" team because it differs from your vision, then you are using, "yes, but" to build a "Yes, And" organization.

That type of hypocrisy won't go unnoticed, and your team will not be invested in following you.

In fact, beware of all "yes, but" driven hypocrisy. As the leader, you are the one most able to say, "yes, but." You will also be the one most tempted to say, "yes, but." While building the "Yes, And" organization you must be the example that others follow, not the exception to the rule.

4. **Be Forgiving**. Change takes time, and mistakes and slip-ups happen. When you are building a "Yes, And" team your people will frequently fall back onto "yes, but." This must be corrected so that "Yes, And" becomes a habit. However, don't

For a special free gift, exclusively for book owners, visit: www.SayYesAnd.com/bookgift

be too harsh on people and drive them away in your effort to help them. You won't change decades of automatic "yes, but" habits in a day. Correct people so they can learn, but do it from a "Yes, And" mentality.

5. **Walk the Line Between Memorable and Annoying.** "Say, 'Yes And'" can be a powerful mantra and reminder to the people in your office. It can also, sadly, just get really annoying. Don't run around squawking, "Say, Yes, And" like a parrot until your people get so sick of hearing it they start mocking you for it.

Use understanding, involvement, and other phrases to remind people without making it into a joke. You want people to think positive thoughts when they hear "Yes, And," not of an annoying harpy who picks at everything they say.

6. **Start With Simple Ground Rules**. Once you have introduced the "Yes, And" concept to your team, start with very clear and simple ground rules that everyone can understand and follow. Let people get a feel for how "Yes, And" works before you have them try to apply it to every facet of their work.

As the boss you have the greatest potential of building a true "Yes, And" team. Don't let your over-eagerness get in the way of your progress.

WITH EQUALS

Perhaps you want to build a "Yes, And" organization with your co-workers; people who you have no power over and who have no power over you. You can not dictate policy to these people, so you must start with an open conversation.

Be honest with your co-workers about what you would like to do and why. Since you can't just schedule a meeting to talk with everyone about it, you will have to approach people one-on-one, or in small groups.

People fear change, so don't jump right in with the idea of, "let's change everything!" That will just scare people and elicit their "yes, but" response. Instead, start by sharing your personal experience with "Yes, And." Make it conversational, and begin with how "Yes, And" has been helping you.

Once people are familiar with your "Yes, And" mindset, you can suggest everyone try applying it in one instance or in one area of focus. For example, before a meeting you could say, "I have an idea that I think will help us get more done in less time." (putting your suggestion in terms of saving time is a great way to get buy-in). "While we're brainstorming, let's all try to say, "Yes, And" instead of "yes, but" as much as possible."

Keep it small and safe and let people see the benefit of it before you start trying to roll it out everywhere. Eventually, once people see how effective, "Yes, And" is, you can start introducing it to more people and groups.

Two more ideas:

1. **Start with a few like minded people.** When affecting this kind of change, a good idea is to seek out the people who are most likely to embrace the "Yes, And" idea first. Get them on board so that when you start suggesting it to others you will have people to back you up and say, "that's a great idea!" Actually, they should say, "Yes, that's a great idea, And let's all do it!"

   This means that if your best friend in the office is a big, "yes, butter," he may not be the best person to start with.

2. **Go to the boss first**. Of course the easiest way to create the "Yes, And" team is to get your boss on board. If you think she'll be open to it, you could have some conversations with her about what "Yes, And" is all about, how it could help the organization, and what the best strategy for getting the whole group on board would be. Just because it's your idea doesn't mean that you have to do it alone. Get your boss on board and you're halfway there.

WITH SUPERIORS

The most difficult challenge is when people above you - your bosses and your bosses' bosses - are "yes, but" people. You don't have the authority to say, "do it this way!" You don't necessarily have the relationship and equal footing to make suggestions. You may even have a very cynical, closed-minded boss who will have no interest in your recommendations.

Here are some suggestions on how to affect change in those environments:

1. **Have an open conversation**. You may be very fortunate and have a boss who is open-minded, willing to listen and try new things, and respects you as someone who can bring him ideas. If so, he may very well already be a "Yes, And" person! In this case, you'll just have to talk directly with him about bringing "Yes, And" to others. However, if you aren't so fortunate and your boss isn't an open-minded "Yes, And" person, this will be harder. But it's still worth trying to have an open conversation about what "Yes, And" is and how it can benefit your team, department, or organization. If you try this, have specific items to implement. Don't just walk in and say, "I want us to be more 'Yes, And!'" That will be met with a blank stare. Rather, say, "I propose at every meeting this month, we designate 10 minutes of 'Yes, And' time for brainstorming new ideas, during which no one is allowed to say, 'no' or 'but.'" Specific plans are much easier to discuss and get implemented than vague goals.

2. **Talk in terms of results and benefits**. Let's be honest: Saying "Yes, And" can sound like an airy-fairy, feel-good, positive-thinking sort of approach to business. As such, hard-nosed managers with an eye on the bottom line don't want to hear about your two-word technique to make people feel better. They want results! Approach them from the benefits they and the organization

as a whole will receive by making "Yes, And" part of the corporate culture. Talk about the benefit to sales, service, and efficiency. It may not work, or it may take time, but you'll get a lot farther talking in terms of tangible results than you will talking about how everyone will "get along better."

3. **Don't "yes but" a "yes butter."** If the people you are talking to are "yes, butters," don't argue with them by responding with "yes, buts." You have to be skilled at responding to their "yes, buts" with your own "Yes, Ands." It takes practice to get good at it, but it's the only way you'll make headway with a "yes, butter."

4. **Play the game**. Chances are, your organization has a game; an unwritten system by which change gets implemented and things get done. Maybe it involves talking first to a specific person. Maybe it involves bringing things up at a certain meeting, or time of day. Maybe you have to prepare a certain kind of presentation. It may not be fair, but if that's the way it is, you have two options:
   a) **Learn the game, and then play it**
   b) **Refuse to play the game, and be frustrated**
   If you are serious about building a "Yes, And" organization, you'll go with the first option.

5. **Set an example**. Regardless of your position in the organization, one of the best ways to affect change is to first do what you propose yourself, and then have people ask you, "how do you do that so well?" If you are a manager with just three employees, make your group a "Yes, And" quartet. Get great results using "Yes, And," and then take it beyond. If you have no one working for you, resolve to apply "Yes, And" just to your own tasks. Produce great results, get great

reviews, become the "go to" person, and then talk to your supervisor about how everyone at the company can get the same results.

I'm not going to lie or oversimplify. Building a "Yes, And" organization when you are not in a position of authority can and will be a tough road. But it will be well worth it. Not only will the organization get better, but you'll be right at the center of the improvement. And that kind of work usually gets noticed…

YES, AND
GO DO IT!

And so we come, not to the end, but to the beginning.

This is your beginning for a new way to approach work, business, relationships, and life.

Life is short. Every time a day ends it's gone forever.

Every time you say "yes, but" you put off living your life to its fullest for a little while longer. Then a little while longer. Then a little while longer. Until eventually you wake up and say with despair, "My God, what have I done!?"

Your "Yes, Ands" don't need to be huge, Earth-shattering decisions (though they can be). It all starts with the little "Yes, Ands" you make every day. Condition yourself to think and say "Yes, And," and eliminate as many "yes, buts" from your life as you can.

Over time it becomes automatic, and you start finding, pursuing, and attracting new opportunities to you every day.

Every time you say, "Yes, And" you take a little step forward. You grow just a little. You create space for new and better opportunities. The next time you say it, you grow and expand a little more. Then a little more. Then a little more. Until eventually you wake up, smile, and say with joy, "My God, what have I done?"

It's just two little words that can make all the difference.

There's nothing more to say. It's up to you now.

Go ahead. Say, "Yes, And." See where it takes you, and enjoy the journey…

REVIEW, SHARE, TWEET

Did you enjoy and find value in "Say, 'Yes, And!'"? If so, please let others know:

Review — Whether you bought the physical version or Kindle version, please take one minute to write a short review on Amazon.com.

Share — Let your Facebook friends know by posting a status update about "Say, 'Yes, And'!" Also, "Like" our Facebook page at SayYesAndFaceBook.com.

Tweet — Get all your Twitter followers on board by Tweeting about the book. Use hashtag #sayyesand.

BRING THE POWER OF "YES, AND" TO YOUR ORGANIZATION!

Do want your entire company, association, or organization to benefit from the immense power of saying, "Yes, And"? Then let Avish bring the power of "Yes, And!" to your group.

For more information about his speaking, training, and consulting options, visit www.SayYesAnd.com.

VOLUME ORDERS

Do you know a group of people that could all benefit from learning about "Yes, And"? Perhaps your team, department, company, association, church, school, volunteer group, service club, professional or trade organization, or friends and family?

Why not buy them all their own copy of, "Say, 'Yes, And!'"?

For information on volume orders, visit www.SayYesAnd.com

ABOUT AVISH

Avish Parashar is an experienced, innovative, energetic, and humorous speaker who uses his 20+ years of experience performing, teaching and studying improv comedy to show organizations and individuals how to deal with the unexpected quickly, effectively, and with a sense of humor.

Avish is the author of "Improvise to Success!" and has created dozens of other products on applying improv skills to business and life.

For more information, please contact Avish directly:
484-366-1793
avish@avishparashar.com
www.SayYesAnd.com

23927927R80055

Made in the USA
Charleston, SC
09 November 2013